A New True Book

WETLANDS

By Emilie U. Lepthien
and
Joan Kalbacken

CP CHILDRENS PRESS ®
CHICAGO

Arrowhead plants grow in wetlands throughout North America.

Library of Congress Cataloging-in-Publication Data

Lepthien, Emilie U. (Emilie Utteg)
  Wetlands / by Emilie U. Lepthien and Joan Kalbacken.
    p.   cm. — (A New true book)
  Includes index.
  Summary: Describes various types of wetlands, their ecological importance, and the plants and animals found there.
  ISBN 0-516-01334-3
  1. Wetlands—Juvenile literature. 2. Wetland ecology—Juvenile literature. 3. Wetland conservation—Juvenile literature. [1. Wetlands. 2. Wetland ecology. 3. Ecology. 4. Conservation of natural resources.] I. Kalbacken, Joan. II. Title.
QH87.3.L47 1993   92-35051
333.91′8—dc20   CIP
                          AC

PHOTO CREDITS

© Reinhard Brucker—44 (top)

© Cameramann International, Ltd.—35, 36 (right)

© John Elk III—6 (bottom), 15, 32, 44 (center)

© Virginia R. Grimes—44 (bottom)

H. Armstrong Roberts—© W. Metzen, 28; © R. Lamb, 41; © Geisser, 42 (top)

© Emilie Lepthien—5, 16

North Wind Pictures—6 (top)

Odyssey/Frerck/Chicago—© Robert Frerck, 10

Photri—20 (top left)

© Carl Purcell—27, 34 (left)

Root Resources—© Kohout Productions, Cover; © Mary A. Root, 9 (top); © Stan Osolinski, 11; © Kitty Kohout, 20 (bottom); © Sandy Nykerk, 26 (left); © Jim Nachel, 30; © Grace L. DeWolf, 39 (bottom)

© James P. Rowan—24

Tom Stack & Associates—© Milton Rand, 9 (center); © Brian Parker, 20 (top right), 23 (right); © Matt Bradley, 22; © Thomas Kitchin, 43

U.S. Fish and Wildlife Service/Courtesy of Stamp King—36 (left)

© Lynn M. Stone—26 (right), 29, 33, 39 (top)

Tony Stone Worldwide/Chicago—© Raymond G. Barnes, Cover Inset; © James P. Rowan, 2

SuperStock International, Inc.—© Ernest Manewal, 17; © E. Carle, 34 (right); © G. Ahrens, 45

U.S. Department of the Interior Fish & Wildlife Service—42 (bottom)

Valan—© Robert Galbraith, 4; © Denis W. Schmidt, 9 (bottom); © S.J. Krasemann, 12; © Robert C. Simpson, 20 (center right); © Val & Alan Wilkinson, 20 (center left); © Ian Davis-Young, 23 (left); © Kennon Cooke, 25

Tom Dunnington—diagram, 19

Cover: Tamarack Bog in northern Wisconsin

Cover Inset: Canada Geese—Horicon National Wildlife Refuge

TABLE OF CONTENTS

WHAT ARE WETLANDS?

Wetlands are among the most productive areas in the world. Many kinds of plants, birds, fish, insects, and mammals make their homes in wetlands.

This marsh in the Adirondack Mountains, New York, is one type of wetland.

A blue heron looks for food in the wetland along a river.

Wetlands are special places where water controls the environment and the plant and animal life. Some are flooded throughout the year. Other wetlands are dry part of the year. Some wetlands have water near the surface of the land.

5

Above: An Atlantic Ocean tidal marsh at the Rachel Carson Wildlife
Refuge in Maine. Below: A coastal estuary in South Carolina

KINDS OF WETLANDS

Two kinds of wetlands are saltwater wetlands. One kind is found along seacoasts. There, mangrove forests and grasses protect the shoreline from erosion.

The second kind of saltwater wetland is called an estuary. Estuaries form at the mouths of rivers. At high tide, salty seawater flows upstream a short distance and mixes with fresh river water.

Plants, fish, and animals that can live in fresh, brackish (slightly salty), or salt water are found in the bays and lagoons of estuaries. Tidal marshes and mangrove swamps develop in these coastal wetlands.

Freshwater wetlands are found around lakes and ponds, along rivers and streams, and in marshy areas, including bogs and swamps. The plants, fish, and animals that live in these wetlands need fresh water.

Wetlands provide homes for many kinds
of wildlife, such as herons and
ibis (above), freshwater clams (left),
and muskrats (below).

Wetland area near Boyne Mountain in the Upper Peninsula of Michigan

Forest wetlands are found along slow-moving rivers. Cottonwood trees, willows, and silver maples thrive in the silty soil deposited by the rivers.

In the southeastern United States, bald cypress, oak,

and ash trees grow in the
forest wetlands.

Pothole wetlands are
found in North Dakota, South
Dakota, and Oklahoma.
They are dry part of the year.
Pothole wetlands provide
food and shelter for waterfowl.

A pothole wetland in Washington State

Small shrubs such as this red bearberry grow on the treeless tundra.

Alaska has almost 63 percent of United States wetlands. About 45 percent of this land is tundra—low, treeless plains covered with black mucky soil.

VANISHING WETLANDS

For many years people did not realize the importance of wetlands. These areas were thought to be dangerous and insect-ridden. Millions of acres were drained for use as farmland. Other wetlands were drained to build housing developments, shopping malls, highways, and railroads. In Iowa, 95 percent of the state's marshes have been lost.

The U. S. Fish and Wildlife
Service studied the loss of
wetlands in the lower 48
states. From the mid-1950s
to the mid-1970s, a total of
4,580,000 acres was
destroyed. Also, pollution
damage decreased the
quality of some wetlands.
By the year 2000, the United
States may lose another
4,250,000 acres of wetlands.

Many fish caught by commercial fishermen breed in saltwater wetlands. These boats fish the waters near Tybee Island, Georgia.

WETLANDS ARE IMPORTANT

Today, people realize that wetlands must be protected. They provide habitat, or places for plants and animals to live. The fish needed by commercial fisheries thrive in their waters.

15

Forest wetland in Florida. In most wetlands
the water level changes throughout the year.

Wetlands also help
prevent flooding. When
rivers and streams overflow
their banks, wetlands
provide a storage place for
floodwater. This prevents soil
16 erosion.

WETLAND ECOSYSTEMS

Wetland soil is different from the soil in dry, upland areas. Rivers and streams carry material washed down from drier land. When this material settles on the bottom, it is called sediment. The sediment mixes with decomposed leaves. The resulting rich soil supports

Wetlands along the Gansu River in China. The land here is 12,000 feet above sea level.

many plants. A healthy food chain develops.

An ecosystem includes all of the plants and animals living in an area. The plants and animals in an ecosystem are dependent on one another.

Each type of wetland has a different ecosystem. But plants are important in all systems. They provide food for many animals living in the ecosystem. However, not all of the plants are eaten.

When plants die, they
fall to the bottom of the
wetland. The plant material
decomposes and makes
nutrients that help other
plants grow.

19

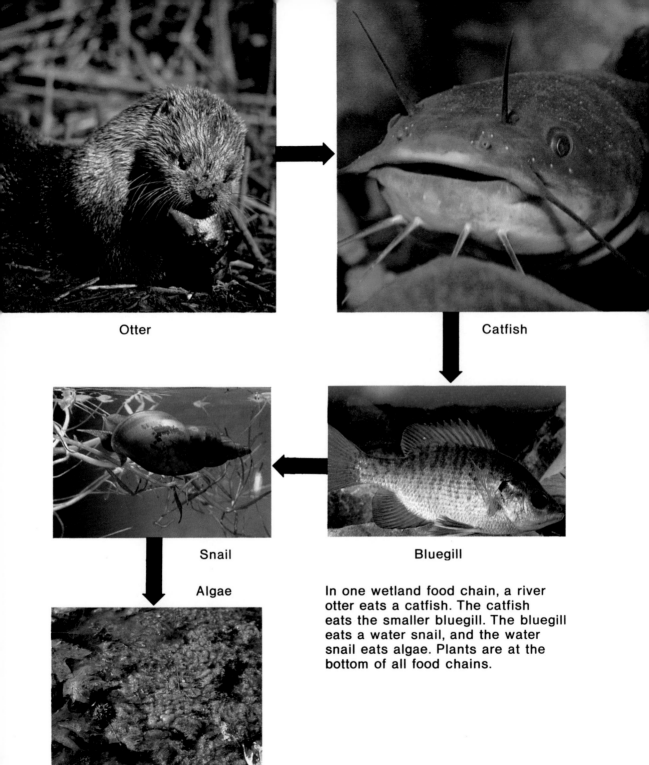

Otter

Catfish

Snail

Bluegill

Algae

In one wetland food chain, a river otter eats a catfish. The catfish eats the smaller bluegill. The bluegill eats a water snail, and the water snail eats algae. Plants are at the bottom of all food chains.

THE FOOD CHAIN

Food chains are very important in a wetland ecosystem. For example, algae are eaten by snails, aquatic insects, and tadpoles. They, in turn, are eaten by small fish. Larger fish, snakes, turtles, and waterfowl are the next link. They feed on the small fish. Muskrats, mink, and other mammals are at the top of the food chain.

THE FISHING INDUSTRY

At least 200 kinds of fish depend on fresh and saltwater wetlands for feeding, spawning, and survival.
    Shellfish and other fish need coastal wetlands. Loss of this habitat has cost the

Fishing for oysters in the coastal waters of Florida

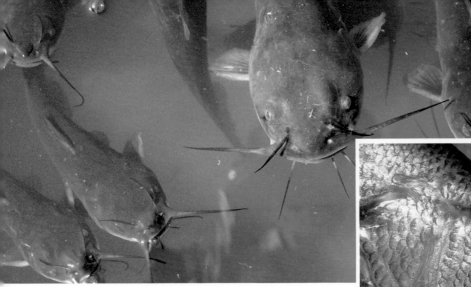

Catfish (above) and crappies (right) find food and safety in the waters of wetlands.

commercial fishing industry $10 billion a year. Sport fishermen also enjoy fishing along coastal wetlands and estuaries.

Inland wetlands provide homes for catfish, bass, crappies, sunfish, and bluegills.

23

Canada geese and mallard ducks rest and feed in wetlands during migration.

WILDLIFE

Birds also depend on wetlands. During migration, ducks and geese feed and rest in marshy wetlands. Many species of birds breed, feed, and find shelter in the rich plant growth near shore.

Almost all of the 4 million wood ducks and 2.5 million mallard ducks that use the Mississippi Flyway spend the winter in southern bottomland forests and marsh wetlands. About 150 other species of birds also depend on these wetlands.

The male wood duck, on the left, is more brightly colored than the female, on the right.

Black bear (above) and deer (right)
are found in wetland areas.

Muskrats, otters,
raccoons, bobcats, black
bears, and deer are found in
wetlands. At least one-third
of America's threatened or
endangered animal species
live in wetland areas.

The spreading roots of mangrove trees catch and hold small particles of silt and sand carried by the water. This helps build up areas of dry land.

MANGROVES

Mangroves are sometimes called "walking trees." The branches of the red mangrove put down roots that prop the tree up out of the water. Mangroves thrive in salt water. Mangrove forests grow

Wood storks make their nests in mangrove trees.

along the southern coastal
areas of the United States.
They provide shelter for
small fish and shellfish. Their
branches provide nesting
places for coastal birds.

When strong winds, high
waves, and hurricanes
strike, mangroves protect

the uplands of Florida and the Gulf Coast.

Unfortunately, in some areas almost 50 percent of these trees have been destroyed. In the United States, they were cut to give people easy access to the ocean.

Many mangrove forests have been destroyed.

Red mangroves growing in the Florida Everglades. There are fifty species of mangroves throughout the world.

Today there is a growing awareness of the importance of mangrove forests. Mangroves prevent shoreline erosion and protect land during storms. New laws have been passed to stop mangrove destruction.

WATER PURIFICATION

Scientists have found that wetlands also help purify our water supply.

Water is purified in wetlands as it soaks into the soil. It is cleaned even more as it filters through porous rock and sand. Without the cleaning process of nature's wetlands, people must build more water-treatment facilities. Without wetlands to take in floodwaters, more flood control projects must be built.

Bald cypress trees grow in soil that is covered
by shallow water in Big Cypress Swamp.

BIG CYPRESS NATIONAL PRESERVE AND THE EVERGLADES

Big Cypress National Preserve is part of the Big Cypress Swamp in southern Florida. Bald and dwarf cypress trees, hardwoods, mangrove forests, and tall grasses grow here.

Alligators, deer, bald eagles, herons, egrets, and the endangered Florida panther live in Big Cypress Swamp. The swamp is the major source of water for the Everglades.

The Florida panther lives in swampy areas of southern Florida. This big cat is related to the cougar, or mountain lion, of western North America.

The watery Everglades (right) is the home of the American alligator (inset). These huge reptiles grow up to twelve feet long.

Everglades National Park lies southeast of Big Cypress National Preserve. It is North America's largest subtropical wilderness. The Everglades has a rainy summer season and a dry winter period. Its plants and animals have adapted to this cycle.

But the Everglades is endangered by land development. People have built canals to drain water from its fragile ecosystem to develop farmland. Efforts are being made to save this remarkable area.

Sign advertising a new housing development in the Everglades area

The money from Migratory Bird Hunting Stamps (left) is used to buy land to prevent wetland areas from being used for housing developments such as this one near Orlando, Florida.

PROTECTING THE WETLANDS

In 1903, the U.S. Congress recognized that too many acres of wetlands had already been lost. Pelican Island in Florida was established as the nation's first refuge in the National Wildlife Refuge System. Then in 1929, the Migratory Bird Conservation Act authorized the saving of wetlands for waterfowl. However, no money was provided to purchase the land.

Since 1934, the Migratory Bird Hunting Stamp Act requires all waterfowl hunters to purchase a stamp each year. Money from the sale of these stamps is used to buy or lease land for waterfowl. By the 1990s more than 440 National Wildlife Refuges had been established.

In 1986, the United States and Canada agreed to a waterfowl management plan. The North American Wetlands Conservation Act supports bird migration projects in the United States, Canada, and Mexico.

Waterfowl depend on wetlands for raising their young.
Above: A Florida sandhill crane and her chick hunt for food
in the water. Below: A pair of herons build their nest.

In 1989, the U.S. government expanded the definition of a wetland. However, new 1991 rules would again leave millions of acres without federal protection. Environmentalists are concerned about this change in wetland policy. Without government support, wetland conservation programs cannot succeed.

WHY WETLANDS NEED OUR HELP

The quality, as well as the quantity, of the world's wetlands must be preserved. The amount of chemicals a wetland can process is limited. Runoffs from urban areas—oil, pesticides, and

Chemical pollution from a factory pours into the waters of a wetland.

A mallard duck (above)
swims in water polluted
by trash and chemicals.
These pelicans (left) have been
coated with oil from
an oil spill.

industrial waste–harm
wetlands. Chemical
drainage from agricultural
lands damages wetlands
where migratory birds and
other animals find food and
shelter.

Once wetlands are lost, it

These barrels of chemicals have been dumped
into a pond where raccoons go to drink.

The Okefenokee Swamp (above) covers a large
area in northern Florida and southern Georgia.
Beautiful wildflowers such as the blue flag
(left) and the marsh marigold (top right)
grow in wetlands.

is expensive to replace them.
People must recognize the
importance of protecting
and restoring the world's
wetlands. Through careful
recycling of waste oil,
plastics, and grass and yard
waste, we can all help protect
these valuable lands.

WORDS YOU SHOULD KNOW

agricultural (ag • rih • KUL • cher • ul) — used for farming

algae (AL • jee) — tiny plants that live in water

aquatic (ah • KWAH • tik) — living in water

authorize (AW • ther • ize) — to give someone the power or permission to do something

bog (BAWG) — spongy, wet ground

brackish (BRAK • ish) — slightly salty

commercial (kuh • MER • shil) — done for a profit or to make a living

contaminate (kon • TAM • in • ayt) — to make dirty or poisonous

decompose (dee • kum • POHZ) — to decay; to break down into its parts

ecosystem (EE • koh • siss • tem) — all the living things in a certain area

endangered (en • DAYN • jird) — in danger of dying out

environment (en • VY • rin • ment) — the things that surround a plant or an animal; the lands and waters of the Earth

environmentalists (en • VY • run • MEN • tuh • lists) — people who study the environment and work to protect it

erosion (ee • ROH • zhun) — the wearing away of land, caused by the action of wind and water

estuary (ES • choo • air • ee) — a wide river mouth

food chain (FOOD CHAYN) — a relationship among living things in which each feeds on a plant or an animal below it in the chain and is eaten in turn by an animal above it

habitat (HAB • ih • tat) — home; the place where an animal usually lives

hurricane (HUR • ih • kayn) — a strong storm with heavy rain and very high winds

lagoon (lah • GOON) — a shallow, salty pond near the seashore

mammal (MAM • il) — one of a group of warm-blooded animals that have hair and nurse their young with milk

mangrove (MANG • grohv) — a tree with spreading branches that put down roots

marsh (MARSH) — low-lying land that is covered with shallow water

migration (MY • gray • shun) — travel, usually for a long distance, to find better food or better weather conditions

nutrients (NOO • tree • ints) — materials in the soil that help plants grow

pesticides (PES • tuh • syds) — chemicals used to kill harmful insects

pollution (puh • LOO • shun) — the dirtying of the Earth's air, water, and land

porous (POR • us) — having many tiny holes so that water can seep through

productive (pro • DUK • tiv) — supporting many different kinds of living things

purification (pyoor • ih • fih • KAY • shun) — cleaning; the removing of chemicals and other harmful materials

refuge (REF • yooj) — a safe place

runoff (RUN • off) — water that runs off the land into lakes and streams

sediment (SEHD • ih • mint) — material that is carried along by water and then deposited on a river or lake bottom

shellfish (SHELL • fish) — animals such as clams and crabs that live in water and have a shell around their body

silty (SIL • tee) — having very small soil particles

spawning (SPAWN • ing) — laying eggs

subtropical (sub • TRAH • pik • uhl) — having a warm and moist climate, almost like tropical areas

swamp (SWAHMP) — an area of low-lying land in which water collects

tundra (TUN • drah) — low, treeless plains covered with black, mucky soil

waterfowl (WAW • ter • fowl) — birds that live on or near water

wilderness (WIL • der • ness) — a natural area without towns or farms

INDEX

About the Authors

Emilie U. Lepthien received her BA and MS degrees and certificate in school administration from Northwestern University. She taught upper-grade science and social studies, wrote and narrated science programs for the Chicago Public Schools' station WBEZ, and was principal in Chicago, Illinois, for twenty years. She received the American Educator's Medal from Freedoms Foundation.

She is a member of Delta Kappa Gamma Society International, Chicago Principals' Association, Illinois Women's Press Association, National Federation of Press Women, and AAUW.

Joan Formell Kalbacken earned a BA in Education from the University of Wisconsin, Madison and an MA from Illinois State University, Normal, Illinois. She was a secondary school teacher in Beloit, Wisconsin, and Pekin and Normal, Illinois. She taught French and mathematics for twenty-nine years, and received the award for excellence in Illinois' program, "Those Who Excel."

She is past state president of the Delta Kappa Gamma Society International and a member of Pi Delta Phi, Kappa Delta Pi, AAUW, and Phi Delta Kappa.